Cricut Easypress Mini for Beginners

The Simplest Ways to Make the Best of Easypress Mini Cricut with Project Ideas

Tiffany Nicholas

Copyright © 2020 by Tiffany Nicholas

TABLE OF CONTENTS

INTRODUCTION

The Cricut Easypress mini is a heat transfer tiny machine that allows you the freedom to make some small designs with the aid of a Heat Transfer Vinyl (HTV). The Easypress family devices work like magic, as they possess even heat from one edge to another, easy to use controls, and smart features. Unlike iron that has varying temperatures of up to 200°F, thereby having low quality of heat transfer. Iron also creates steam that makes the transfer of heat evenly unsuccessful.

Crafters, including myself, have patiently waited for a small and simple device that will allow us to transfer cuts to small surfaces that include baby shoes, shirts, pockets, hats, small handbag, pillows, papers, backpacks, stuffed animals, headbands, etc. As it has been difficult, putting cuts on such objects when no tool or device will help in making the imaginations become a reality.

Suppose you are new to this fantastic technology (Cricut world). In that case, Easypress family is made up of small heat transfer devices that come with ceramic hotplates, to produce quick, consistent, and professional, flawless vinyl crafts that last longer.

This short guide will reveal the natural and best ways to use the Cricut Easypress mini. Other things that will be covered in this book include:

What you should expect when you purchase this guide Easypress mini.

How to Set the Easypress Mini Temperature.

THE EASYPRESS FAMILY

The Cricut inc created four different types of sizes of Easypress machines that fit a wide range of applications- to achieve significant and bold graphics to small cuts that are flawless and last longer.

Easypress 2 (12" x 10")

Easypress 2 (9" x 9")

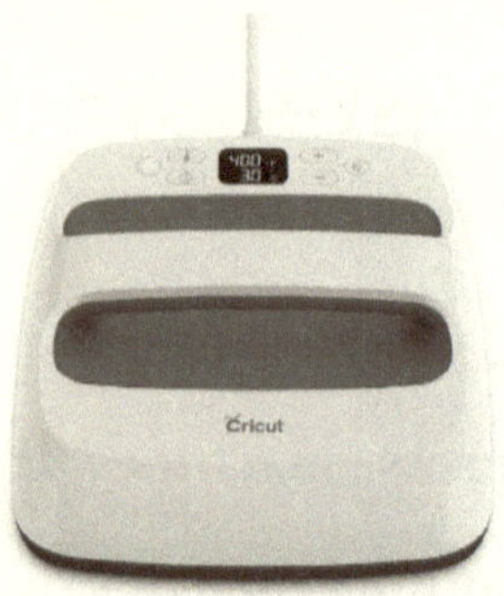

Easypress 2 (6" x 7")

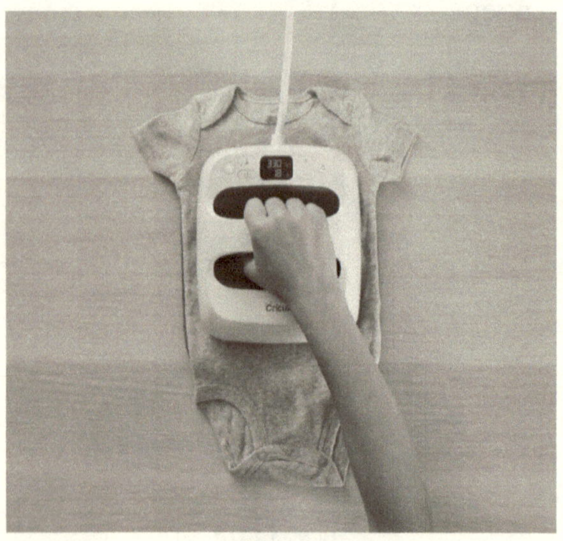

All the above sizes have the following features
and benefits:

All the sizes mentioned above of Easypress Cricut devices are easy, fast, quick transfer to any objects such as jerseys, baby bodysuits, and banners.

1. Latest design of heat plate: Feature number 1 is a ceramic-coated surface with special heating elements that makes the edge-to-edge heat of this device evenly distributed, thereby making your job looks professional.

2. Feature 2: These devices have features that control temperature up to 205° (400°F). Just input your recommended time and temperature settings for the infusible Ink project or HTV and achieve your goals.

3. Safety part: This is an insulated safety base that will protect the work surface. It has been designed to shut off after 20 minutes when not in use.

4. Work section: This is the assembly of your magical device. Use it to design, cut images, and then transfer the cuts to give the perfect project.

Easypress Mini (1.92" x 3.25")

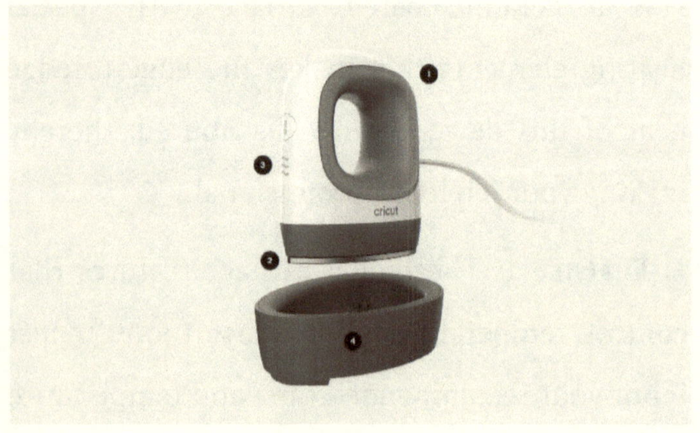

This device is also known as Mini but Mighty

This type of Easypress Cricut is a tiny professional heat transfer device that beats your imaginations!

Features and Benefits:

1. **Shape:** This mini has a perfect shape of 1.92" wide and 3.25" height.

2. **Advanced heat plate:** This part has an extra layer for protection.

3. **Heat setting controls:** Press the required controls and have the best final project.

4. **Safety feature:** This is an insulated base to protect the work surface. It will shut off the device when inactive for 13 minutes.

UNBOXING THE EASYPRESS MINI AND ITS FEATURES

The Easypress mini comes in a tiny white box that has a mini-press and safety base. This type of Easypress Cricut is also known as mini but mighty.

The package:

Before opening

After opening

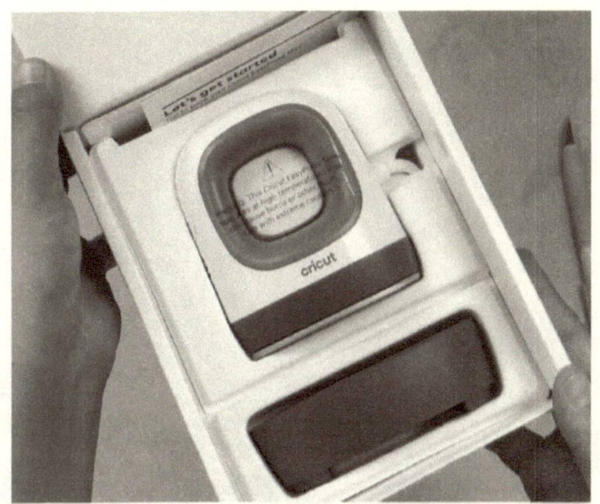

The Safety base

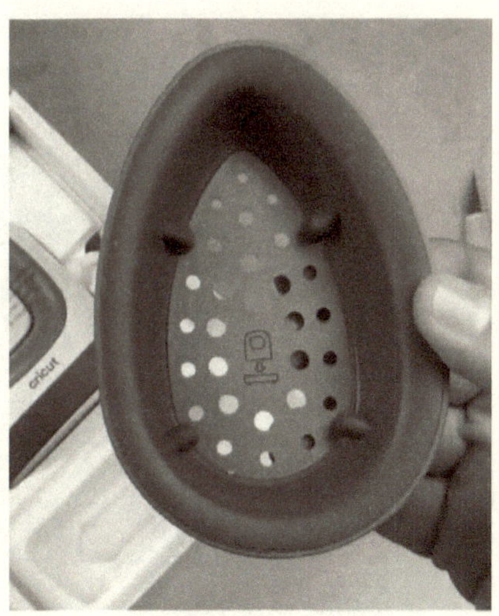

The Extension cord

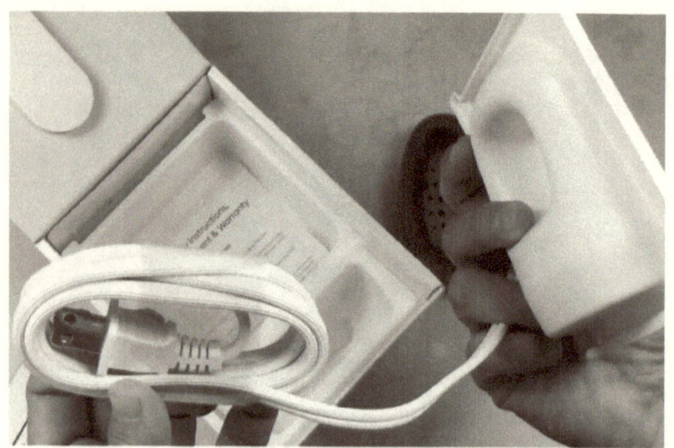

The device

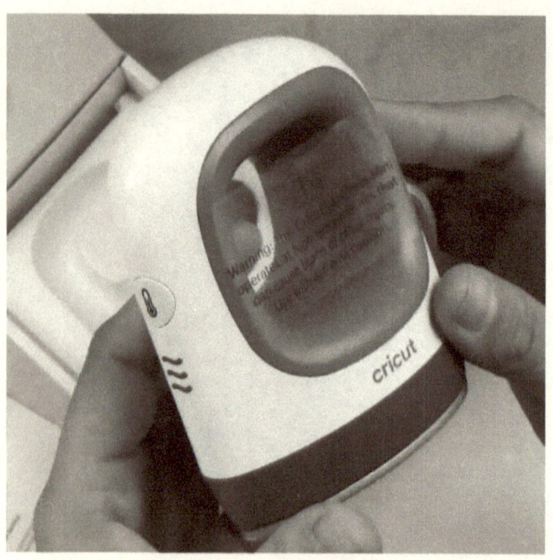

The Assembled Easypress mini

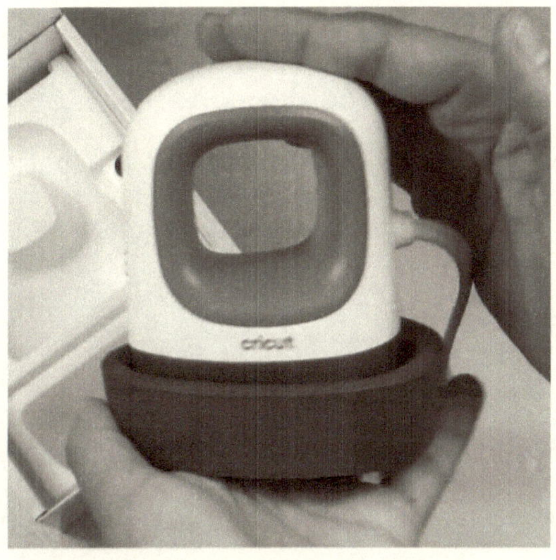

Features and Benefits:

Size and Shape:

This mini has a perfect shape of 1.92" wide and 3.25" height. The base of the device looks exactly like traditional iron and comes with a comfortable handle that will make manipulation of the machine easier.

Heat plate:

The heat plate of Easypress mini is a ceramic coat that allows the device to heat the object evenly and help in the smooth navigation on the purpose of being worked on its surface.

Heating:

The Easypress mini shows its temperature settings. The settings are self-explanatory and can be seen as High, Medium, and Low. For you to choose your recommended heat setting, press the ON-OFF button.

First press on the button is for low heat

The second tap on the button is for medium heat

The third tap on the button is for high heat.

There will be an orange light displayed when the device has reaches the preferred temperature, and the green light will come up when it is at the recommended temperature.

Safety features:

An insulated safety base comes with the package. This part is designed to protect the surfaces of the objects you will be working on. This part is designed in such a way to shut off within 15 minutes when not active.

HOW TO USE THE EASYPRESS MINI

Getting Started

Steps:

1. Remove the device from the package, and plug the extension cord into a wall outlet.

2. Press the power button once on the device.

3. Cycle through different levels.

4. To turn off the device, press the button for the fourth time.

5. Leave the machine in the safe base to heat up.

6. Preheat the blank you are using; the surface is expected to be preheated between 10 to 20 seconds with your device.

7. Transfer the blank to the towel or Easypress mat.

8. Lay the design on the blank.

9. Use resistant tape to hold the design to prevent the design from getting out of alignment.

Press the Easypress machine gently on the material, and apply the pressure to the where the material using the required time.

Note: It doesn't matter the size of the Easypress Cricut; it gets hot and heats up quickly due to its small size. To get to the high setting only takes 60 seconds.

EASYPRESS TEMPERATURE SETTINGS:

The Easypress Cricut devices are designed with three different temperature settings- Low,

Medium, and High.

Low: This setting is meant for delicate or light materials such as foils and sport flex iron-on.

Medium: This temperature setting is recommended for material that is iron-on and glitter.

High: High-temperature setting is ideal for materials that require a high amount of heat, such as infusible transfer sheets, pens, and markers.

Heat Settings	Temperature
High	365 – 371 °F
Medium	305 – 315 °F
Low	268 – 275 °F

HOW TO KNOW THE RECOMMENDED HEAT TRANSFER

We recommend that you make use of the Cricut heat transfer site (https://bit.ly/2PzfsUa)

to determine the heat needed from the three different heat settings (low, medium, or high).

Remember that you have to select the Heat-Transfer Material and also pick the Base Material. Then click on Apply to get the recommended results. These results include how long it will take the device to preheat, the setting of low, or medium, or high temperature to heat. The results will also remind you to make use of light pressure and constant movement.

EASYPRESS MINI TIMER

Look at your device very well, and you will notice that it does not come with a timer. You use separate time devices that are readily available, such as phone, clock, or wristwatch, to know the heating duration.

MATERIALS AND CONSIDERATIONS WITH EASYPRESS MINI

It is important you take note of this advice! The most important thing to remember when using Easypress machines is the guide to heat (https://bit.ly/2PzfsUa).

Previously we discussed how to select your type of machine and the material you want to work with to know the next steps in such a case.

Remember that failure to follow the guide on heat; there will not be a success in the transfer of heat when working on your project.

MATERIALS NEEDED WHEN USING EASYPRESS MINI

Heat resistant tape: You need this tape to

fasting your projects to the surface so it won't be misaligned.

Easypress mat: This mat is used to secure the surface or to press the surface. Mat is very useful whenever you are working with hats.

Heat resistant gloves: These gloves are optional. Some people are afraid of heat whenever they are handling objects that get too hot quickly.

FREE SVG FILES

You may need some SVG files to beautify your projects. Go to the sites provided below and download the files that you want.

Remember that SVG files can only be saved on the computer.

Sites to get free SVG files.

https://www.vecteezy.com/

https://freesvgdesigns.com/

https://freesvgdesigns.com/quote-coffee-then-hustle-free-svg-files-1355/

https://www.creativefabrica.com/freebies/free-crafts/

https://freesvg.org/

Note: Please check if they can be used for commercial purposes.

IS EASYPRESS MINI FOR ME?

There are fundamental questions that need critical answers!

Are you a craft lover?

Do you like to personalize small surfaces so to beautify them?

Are you a creator of mini handcraft objects?

If you say YES to any or all of the above questions, definitely Easypress machines are for you!

Suppose you are the type that loves to design small objects such as doll clothes, shoes, hats, bibs, etc. Then Easypress mini is a device that should be in your collection. If you discover what you can achieve with this excellent tool, you won't consider its price.

The way and easy at which this device evenly distribute heat makes the usage of mini iron to be obsolete. Most times, the mini iron will get smoky and may not distribute the heat evenly.

BEST SURFACES FOR EASYPRESS MINI

The Easypress Mini machine can be used with any iron-on vinyl, infusible Ink, and fusible fabric

The followings are some of the best surfaces that can be decorated using Easypress Mini machine:

Stuffed Animals

Notebooks

Hats

Shoes

Earrings

Doll clothes

Headbands

Eyeglass cases

Small bags

Fabric Pumpkins

Papers

Designs on shirts

Bows

Backpacks

Small pockets

Designs on pillows

Handbags

Pocket tees

And lots more!

Note: As discussed earlier, we recommend that you make use of the Cricut heat transfer site (https://bit.ly/2PzfsUa) to determine the heat needed from the three different heat settings

(Low, medium or high)

PROS AND CONS OF EASYPRESS MINI MACHINE

Below are the pros and cons of Easypress mini machine:

Pros:

Easy to use: With the way this tool is designed, it is straightforward to use. Creating your craft and project will be fun and more comfortable.

Easy to store: It is a small tool that will be easy to store, no matter how congested the storage area is.

Safe: Using the Easypress mini is secured as it is comfortable, and there may not be any accident when handling. Also, remember that the safety base of the device is an additional part of making it safe.

Cons:

Restricted use: This device is meant for small projects, so it will be challenging to use it for big projects.

Expensive: When Easypress mini is compared to other tools that are alternative to it, it can be seen as a little pricey.

Lack of Pressing mat: The package does not contain a pressing mat. And this may discourage some people from purchasing it.

MINI PROJECTS ON EASYPRESS CRICUT

HOW TO USE EASYPRESS MINI TO DECORATE MUG USING HTC VINYL

Materials Needed:

Mug cup

Cricut Easypress mini

HTV Vinyl

Cricut machine (explore or maker)

Weeding tool

Steps:

1. Create a template to be placed on the Mug with a Cricut machine.

2. Pre-warm your Mug.

3. Place the design created on the Mug.

4. Switch your Easypress mini temperature to high temperature and begin to press the design to the Mug until well pasted.

5. Use the weeding tool to remove the vinyl form the cup to leave only the impression of the design.

6. After you have removed the vinyl, place the Mug in the oven at 325°F for 5 minutes.

7. Use alcohol to remove the excess glue.

HOW TO USE EASYPRESS MINI TO DECORATE BABY BIBS

Materials Needed:

Bib

Mat

Cricut Easypress mini

HTV Vinyl

Cricut machine (explore or maker)

Weeding tool

Steps:

1. Create a template to be placed on the bib with the Cricut machine.

2. Pre-warm your bib front and back.

3. Place the design on the bib.

4. Set your timer to 25 seconds.

Note: Check the Easypress heat guide on the level of the heat to set.

5. Then begin to press the design with Easypress mini on the bib for the speculated 25 seconds.

6. Turn to the back of the bib and set your timer to 15 seconds. Then press the back of the

bib with Easypress mini for 15 seconds.

7. Gently remove transparent plastic.

Outcome 2

HOW TO ADD FLOWERS TO YOUR SHOES

Note that all kinds of shoes will work for iron-on vinyl. It can be a sneaker, slip-on the results will be great. The truth is that any shoe made of cloth will work correctly on Easypress mini. This doesn't mean that leather shoes will not work better.

Materials needed:

Easypress mini Cricut

Weeding tools

Hand Towel

Vinyl (iron-on golden and yellow colors)

Cricut Machine (explore or maker)

Shoes

Cricut machine (explore or maker)

Masking tape

Steps:

1. Stuff your hand towel into the shoe to give solid surface when you want to add pressure.

2. Select the medium heat setting on the Easypress mini and your timer to 30 seconds.

3. Create a template to be placed on the shoe with the Cricut machine.

4. Use Easypress mini to warm the surface of the shoe for 15 seconds.

5. Now place the design on the shoe, and use the masking tape to hold it steady on the shoe.

6. Then begin to press the design on the shoe

with Easypress mini for the speculated 30 seconds.

7. Continue with these procedures until you place all the designs on both pairs.

HOW TO PERSONALISE A HAT

Materials Needed:

Easypress Mini

Masking tape

Mat

Hat

Hand towel

Cricut machine (Maker or explore)

HTV Vinyl

Steps:

1. Create a template to be placed on the hat

with the Cricut machine.

2. Set the temperature level of the Easypress mini to low.

3. Preheat your hat for 15 seconds.

4. Use the tape to hold the design on the hat firmly.

5. Stuff the hat with a hand towel to the hat to give a stable surface when you want to add pressure.

6. Then begin to press the design on the hat with Easypress mini for 30 seconds.

7. Remove the transparent plastic.

CONCLUSION

I hope this book has inspired and put you on the right track!

If you have been following this guide from the beginning, you should know that if you can't afford to install standard heat press in your room, the Easypress mini machine and other Easypress machines will be able to do some if not all the job to be done. It is compact, light, and easy to use.

I have used this great device to do some outstanding projects that beat my imaginations.

If you found this guide helpful, do not hesitate to send it to your friends who love homemade crafts or share it with them. Not only are you encouraging them, but you are also supporting my work.

Thanks

Reference

https://cricut.com/en_us/cricut-easypress#how-it-works
works
https://cricut.com/en_us/cricut-easypress-mini.html

Image Credits

www.cricut.com

www.pexels.com

www.ingramcontent.com/pod-product-compliance
Lightning Source LLC
Chambersburg PA
CBHW051129250726
48655CB00007B/2967